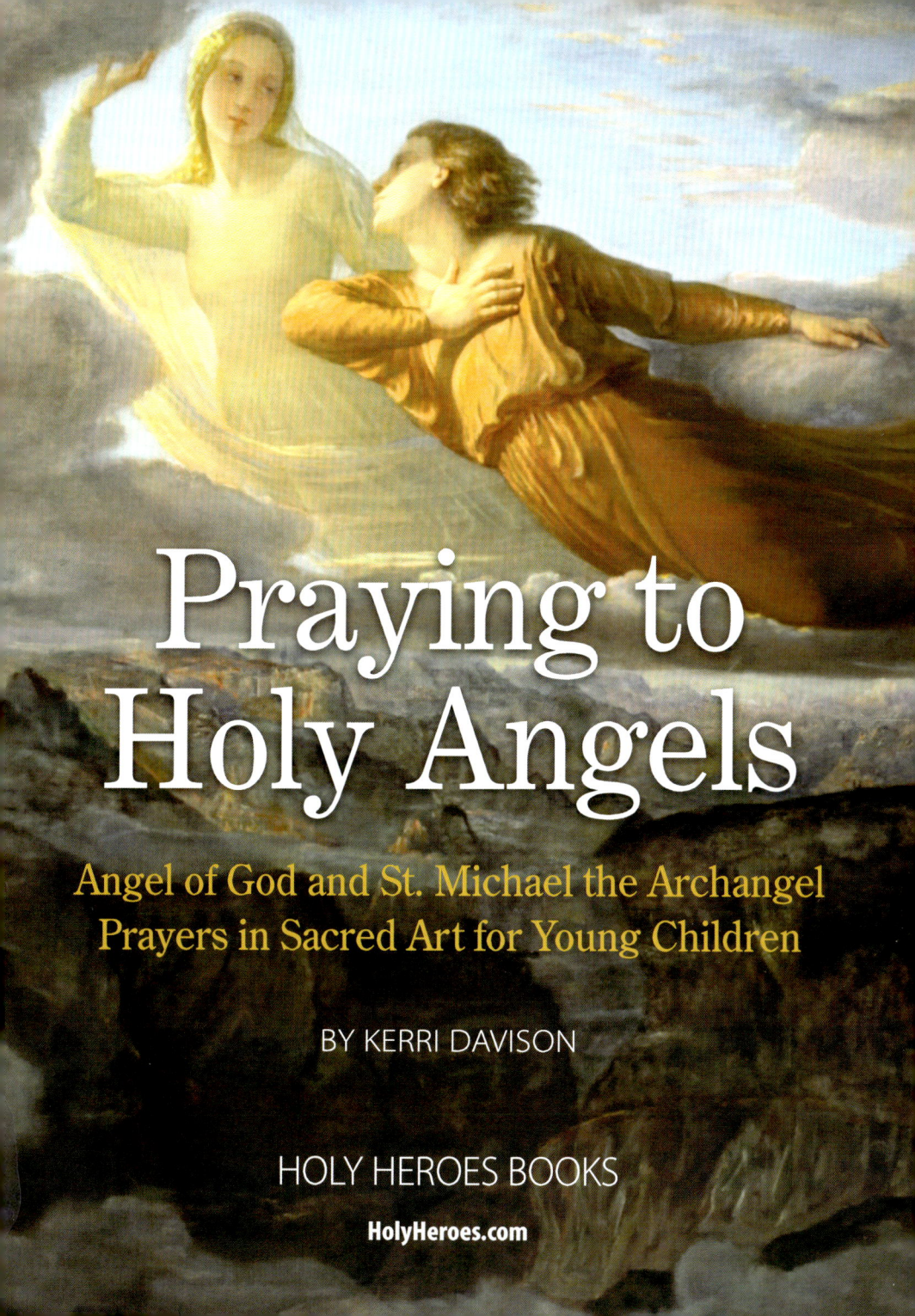

Dedicated with gratitude
to parents and grandparents
who pass on the deep wisdom of the Faith
by reading to little children.

Praying to Holy Angels: Angel of God and St. Michael the Archangel Prayers in Sacred Art for Young Children
Copyright © 2022 Kerri M. Davison.
Published by Holy Heroes, LLC. All rights reserved. No part of this publication may be reproduced or used in any form or by any means—graphic, electronic, or mechanical, including photocopying, recording, or information storage-and-retrieval systems—without permission of the publisher.
Excerpts from the English translation of the *Catechism of the Catholic Church* for use in the United States of America. Copyright ©1994, United States Catholic Conference, Inc.—Libreria Editrice Vaticana. Used with permission.

ISBN 978-1-936330-99-7   Printed in the U.S.A.   **HolyHeroes.com**

A Note to Readers

Angels are a gift from God given to aid us on our way to Heaven. We need to teach children about our angel friends and protectors who are all around us, everywhere, all the time. There is a guardian angel especially made by God for each child—a guardian angel who will never leave his child and is always there to assist and protect him.

Another protector is St. Michael the Archangel, whose name in Hebrew means, "Who is like God?" The answer to this rhetorical question is of course, "No one." And St. Michael showed this when he drove the angels who refused to serve God out of Heaven. Those disobedient angels did not want to serve God, they wanted to be God. St. Michael the Archangel is the protector of all Catholics and of the Catholic Church.

Teaching a child to love and pray to these powerful protectors and guides is one of the greatest gifts you can give to a child.

May God bless you.

From its beginning until death, human life is surrounded by the angels' watchful care and intercession. Beside each believer stands an angel as protector and shepherd leading him to life. Already here on earth the Christian life shares by faith in the blessed company of angels and men united in God. *(Catechism of the Catholic Church 336)*

God made all things in Heaven and on Earth,
all things we can see and those we cannot see.
God first created the angels.
Do you know how you are like an angel?
You have a soul that will live forever,
just like an angel.
However angels do not have a body like you do,
so they cannot be seen, even though
they are always nearby.

Sometimes God allows an angel to be seen, like when the
Archangel Gabriel appeared to the Blessed Virgin Mary
to ask her to be the mother of Jesus.

A long time ago the angels had to choose
whether they would serve God.
The bad angels would not serve God
and that started a great battle
between the good and bad angels.
The good angels won the battle,
and now we call the bad angels demons.
The leader of the bad angels
is called the Devil or Satan.

St. Michael the Archangel led the good angels in battle
and drove the bad angels out of Heaven.

Just as God created each person for a special reason,
God created each angel for a unique purpose.
God created Guardian Angels to protect us from harm
and to inspire us to do good.
There is one Guardian Angel for each person.
Just think: God created your Guardian Angel
before you were even born—He was planning to
create you, so He first created your Guardian Angel!
Your Guardian Angel has always been with you
and will never leave you.

When you die, your Guardian Angel
will accompany you to God where you will be judged
and sent to Heaven, Purgatory, or Hell.

Angels always see God.
Jesus said, "See that you never despise
any of these little ones for I tell you that
their angels in Heaven are continually
in the presence of My Father in Heaven."

(Matthew 18:10)

Pray to your Guardian Angel
anytime you need help,
are confused about what to do,
or are afraid.

The "Angel of God" prayer
is a good one to pray every day.

The Angel of God Prayer

Angel of God

Each of us has a Guardian Angel given to us by God when we were created.

My guardian dear,

Your Angel will stay by your side
for your entire life.

To whom God's love commits me here,

God shows his love for us by giving us an Angel
to be our faithful friend and protector.

Ever this day be at my side,

Your Angel is always with you
and will never leave you.

To light and guard,

Your Guardian Angel protects you,
and offers your prayers and good works to God.

To rule and guide.

Amen.

Your Guardian Angel prays for you and guides you.

The St. Michael the Archangel Prayer

St. Michael the Archangel,

St. Michael the Archangel drove all the bad angels, whom we now call devils, out of Heaven.

Defend us in battle.

The battle is the fight against temptation and sin.

Be our protection against the wickedness and snares of the Devil.

The Devil tries all the time to lead us into sin, and St. Michael can help protect us from the Devil.

May God rebuke him,

Just like St. Michael the Archangel,
we ask God to condemn the Devil.

(Jude 1:9)

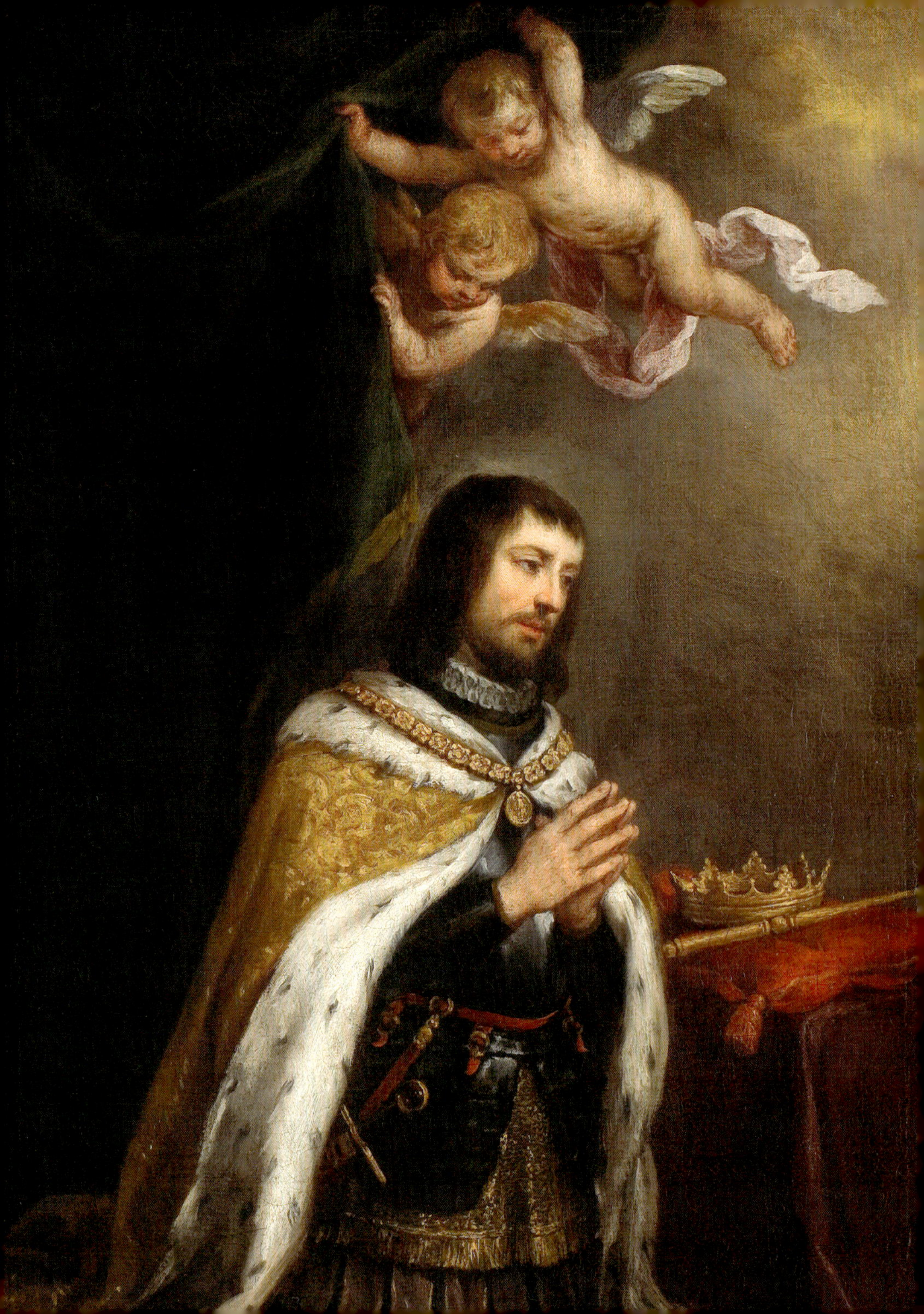

We humbly pray,

We must ask God in prayer for protection.

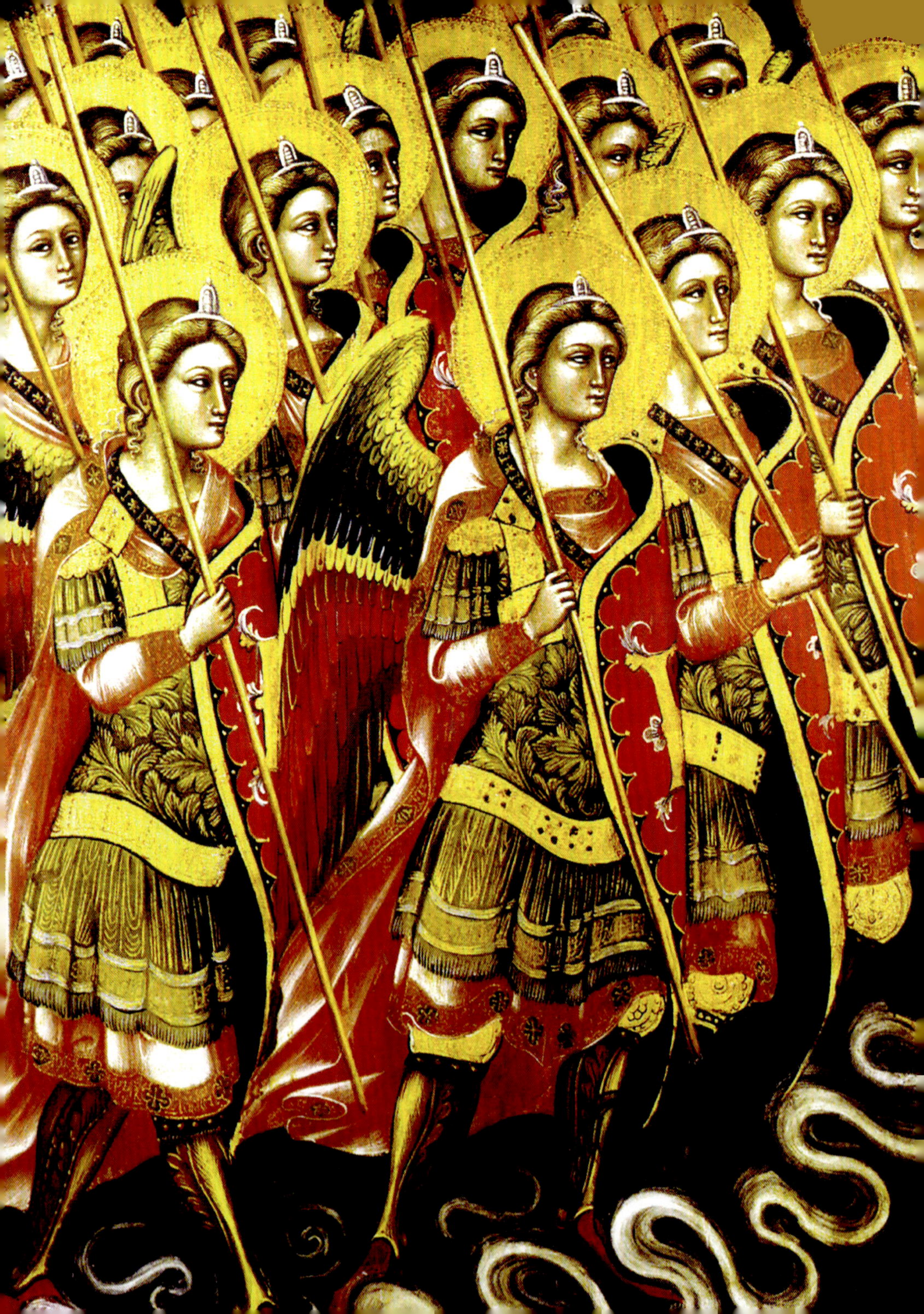

And do thou, Oh Prince of the Heavenly Host,

The Prophet Daniel called St. Michael the Archangel God's "great prince, guardian of Your people." (Daniel 12:1)

The "Heavenly Host" is God's army of angels. (Matthew 26:53)

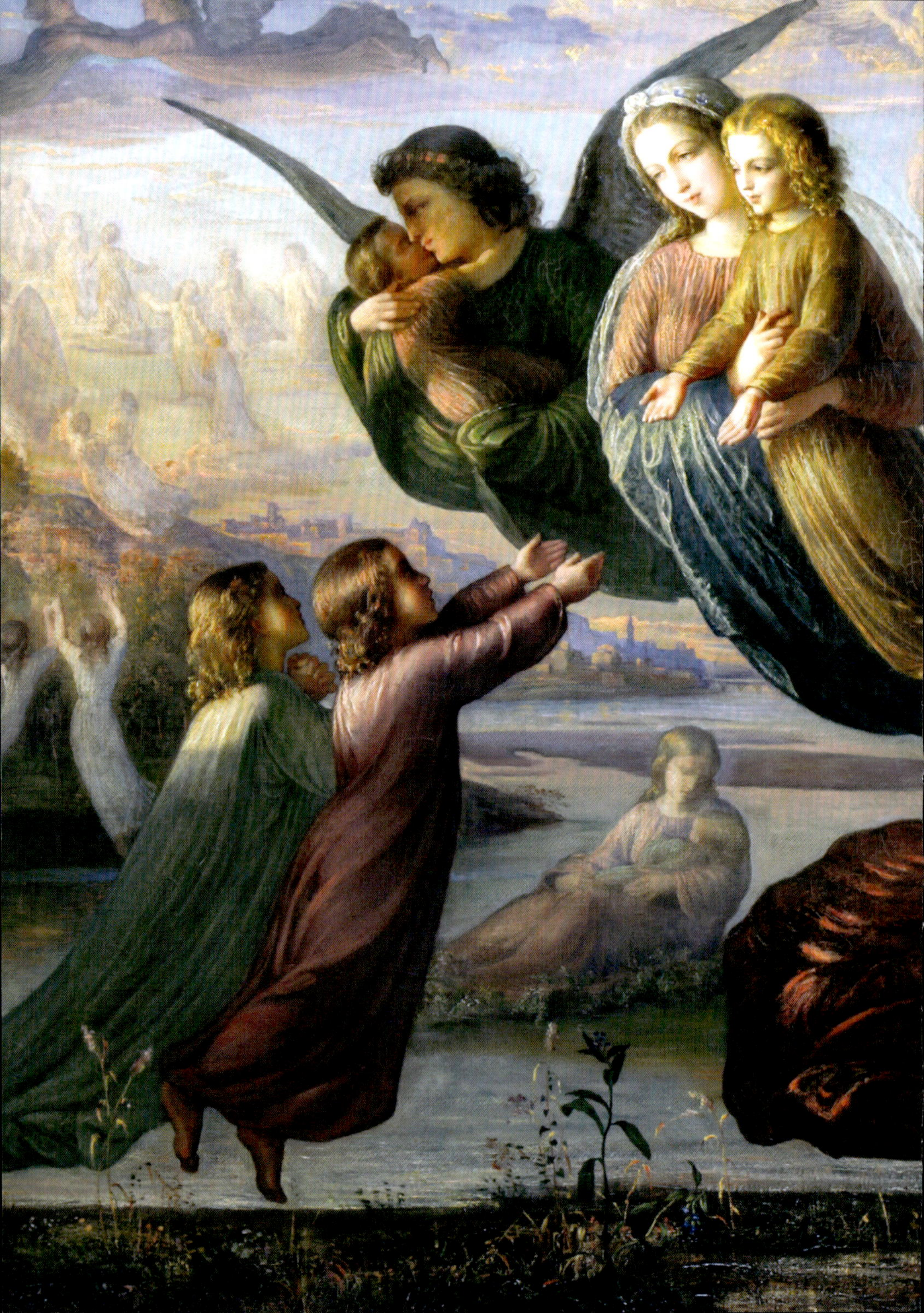

By the power of God

St. Michael the Archangel's power comes from God.

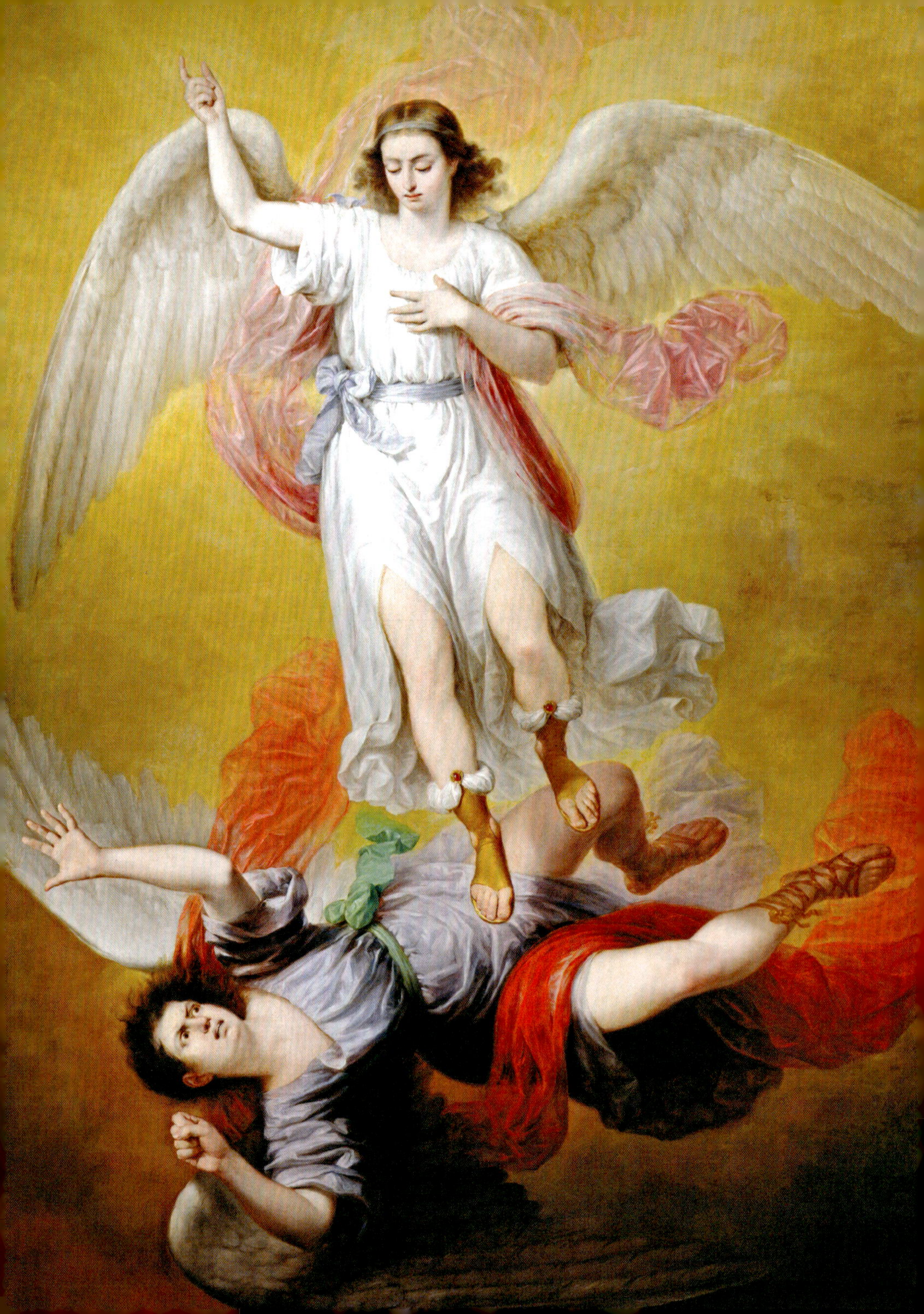

Cast into hell Satan and all the evil spirits

Satan is the chief of all the devils.
He was once an angel but he chose sin instead of God.

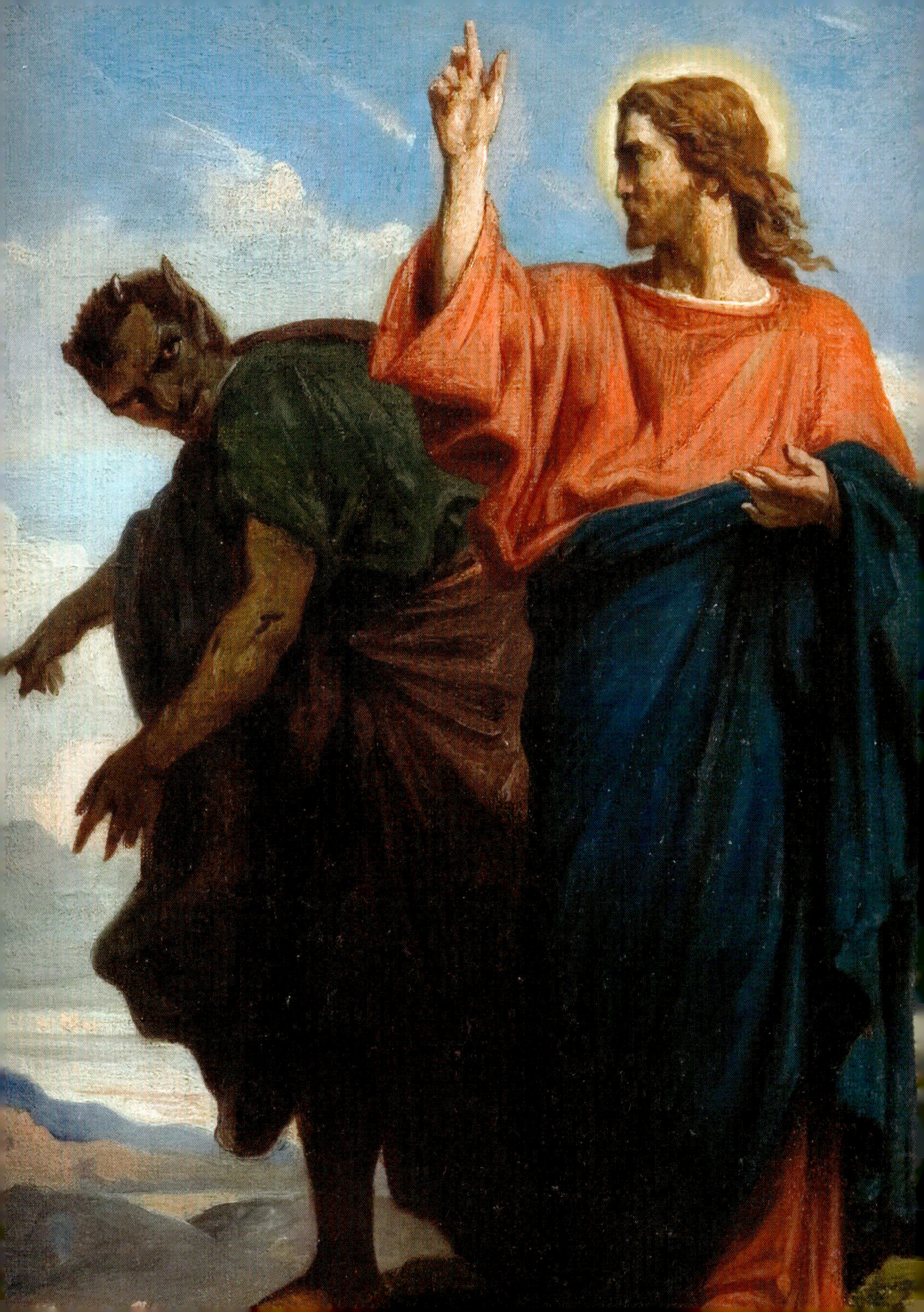

Who prowl about the world seeking the ruin of souls.

Amen.

The Devil is always trying to tempt us to sin because he hates goodness and does not want us to enjoy happiness with God that he has lost forever.

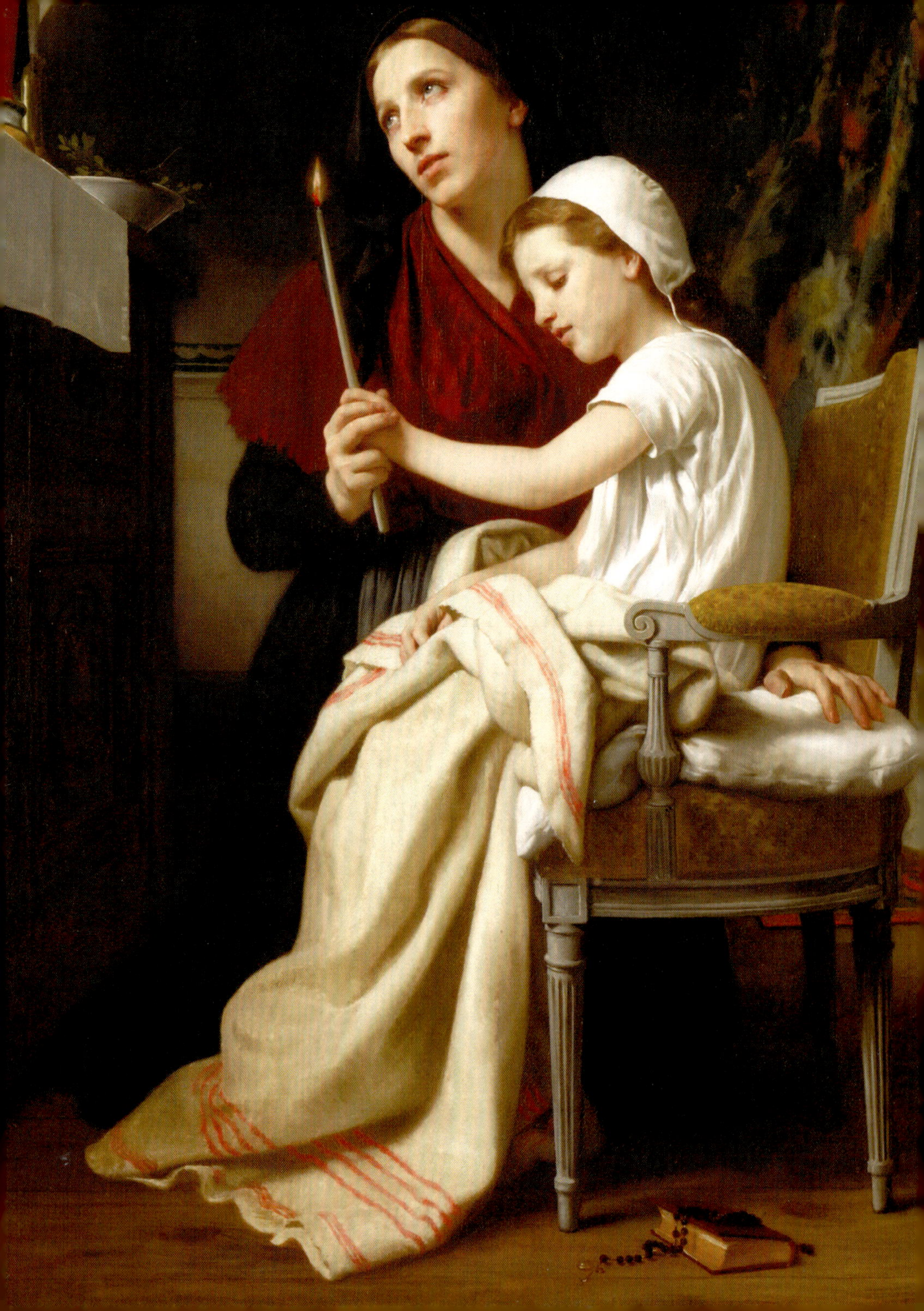

Pray the Guardian Angel and
St. Michael the Archangel
prayers every day
for help and protection.

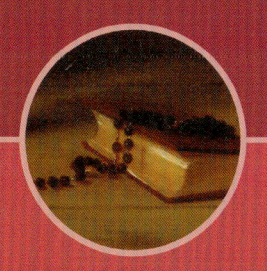

Picture Credits

Title, **Artist**	Page
The Ideal, Janmot	1
Education of the Virgin Mary, Giovanni Romanelli	2
The Passage of Souls, Janmot	3
Guardian Angel, Kaulbach	3
The Guardian Angels, Mann	3
The Annunciation, Murillo	4-5
St. Michael the Archangel, Perugino	6-7
The Passage of Souls, Janmot	8-9
Let the Children Come Unto Me, Vogelstein	10-11
The Golden Ladder, Janmot	12-13
Guardian Angel, Kaulbach	14-15
The Angel and the Mother, Janmot	16-17
Tobias and the Archangel Raphael, Goya	18-19
St. Ann and Our Lady, Murillo	20-21
Guardian Angel, Deken	22-23
Guardian Angel, Fetti	24-25
Fall of the Rebel Angels, Giordano	26-27
St. Michael Trampling the Dragon, Raphael	28-29
St. Michael and the Dragon, Raphael	30-31
Archangel Overwhelming the Demon, Vivarini	32-33
God the Father and the Holy Ghost, Vaccaro	34-35
St. Fernando, Murillo	36-37
The Celestial Army, Arpo	38-39
The Memory of Heaven, Janmot	40-41
The Fall of Lucifer, Esquivel	42-43
The Temptation of Christ by the Devil, Barrias	44-45
The Thanks Offering, Bouguereau	46-47